For Ed, Sari, Mama & Papa Cleod
thank you for showing me the greatest of what ifs
and that every cleod has a silver lining

Scan Me

Use your phone to scan the QR codes throughout and watch the poems come to life. Don't forget to subscribe so you never miss a new poem!

Positive Poetry www.janeymcleod.com

The Gig Prayer

Take the mic through my mouth
And speak your life to their hearts
Take my ego from the floor
And put your strength in my art

POSITIVE POETRY

WORDS OF HOPE

What if
every time you spoke
you had a choice to speak
hope
into another person's
soul?

What is this Book For?

This is for the sad days
For the bad days
For the just woke up not okay days
For the skint days
For the debt days
For the stranger just smiled
It's gonna be okay days

For the days grief feels too giant a mountain to
Swallow
For the hormonal, I just need to sit and wallow
For the just been dumped
For the just been punched
For the dunno how I'm gonna make it to tomorrow

For the
Performed ya first show
For the just diagnosed
For the –
Got engaged today!
For the found a tenner on the floor when you
Prayed today
This is for your birthday
This is for that not sure God can hear me day
For the 'I just wanna crawl outta my body' day

This is for the days you're stood under that tree
That for some reason captures every
Wonderful memory and releases it in the breeze
For the too many soya cappuccino days
For the 'I can't wait tables any longer!'
For the 'I can't wait any longer!'
For the 'I can feel myself getting a little bit
Stronger'

This is for the days you need to know
There is a light inside the tunnel with you
Not just at the end

To know someone is always with you
That someone will never leave you
This is for the 'It's okay I'm not okay
I'm a completely broken mess' kinda day
This is for the day you look at your debris
Say 'Wow I can see light shining through the
Cracks in me'

This is for that day!
This is for that day, you realise that maybe
Everything is going to be okay

Hope Deferred

I'm run down today
Hope deferred makes the heart sick
Choose hope and be well

Get Your Hopes Up

Hope is the seal between your flesh and your
Bones
It's the driving force forwards when you feel like
You can't go
Hope is the bounce that bites BIGGER than you bet
It's the blind faith BARRAGE that tears you out of
The net
Hope is the HEALING that helps HUG all the hurts
It's the rope out of the PIT when you're clawing
Through the dirt
Hope is the LIFE, it's the LIGHT, it's the edge
When you wake
It's the floor beneath your feet by your bed
HOPE is the HAND that reaches out 'cus you know
There's a hand to hold refusing you to GO alone
Hope is a bridge, it's a step, it's the way
When there isn't any other leading to a NEW day
Hope is BEING CERTAIN of the things you cannot
See
It's a WINDOW through the wall of impossibility
Hope is the rope in the pit; GRAB it someday soon
You'll look down
And THANK God you didn't quit

Hope is CONSISTENT when your circumstance
Isn't
It's always in reach though the WORLD says it isn't
Hope soothes shock; it's the rock to climb on
When the time clocks out
When you're blocked in DOUBT!

When I hear my thoughts 'reassure' me with
Don't get your hopes up
I shudder and cringe, *why not?*
I dismiss it as the most twisted concept
I could have thought up
I'm gonna binge on hope like love brought me up
'Cus the things that have broken me, choked me
Smoked me out of my comfort zone
Unveiled opportunity
The situations that surrounded me with loneliness
Reminded me how grounded in community I was
            There is hope.
And though it's travelling at the speed of light to
The highest heights
It's not going anywhere. Hope is always within
Reach. Hope is required. Get your hopes up!

Broken Cities

There are so many broken hearts in broken cities
Broken hearts in broken cities
Fed up worn down
Head in hands in pity
'Cus the day's gone dark in this broken city
In this broken city, this broken city
The days gone dark in this broken city
The hearts are broken in this broken city
The hearts are choking in this broken city
Starved of love in this broken city
But an arm has stretched out in this broken city
It holds the hearts left on the side to die
The orphan hearts, the rejected hearts
The bruised, broken, abused and neglected hearts
The affected hearts, the dissected hearts
The fooled and lied to, stamped on hearts
The grieving hearts, unbelieving hearts
High achieving, perceived as the messed up
Hearts
The striving hearts, the blinded hearts
The trafficked, not eaten, defeated hearts
The addicted, homeless, evicted
The depicted as sick
Tongues rip like they're wicked
But this arm stretched out

Prompts the dark right out
As it burns with light
Fades the coals of doubt
It prompts one heart
To be an outstretched heart
And that outstretched heart
Stretches out
Her arms like arteries
Painting a work of art
But that work of heart sparks
Light in the dark
There's life in her heart
There was an explosion of hell
But these hearts
Are queueing
To give blood to the victims
Homes to the evicted
Give food to the hungry
Set free the addicted
These hearts march on
They'll never stop marching on
'Cus the outstretched arm
Causes love to be done

Twenty First Century Comforts

Soon
When a close friend asks me how I got through
This
        Strangers tweeting comforting birdsong

So many lows where I just wanted to reach for
Help
From anyone, with words so bluntly saying
Do you get this pain? Is this unique to me?
Was it this Hard for you?

I imagined a comforting reply, where I just
Happened to write to the exact right stranger at
The exact right time
Who was going through exactly what I was too
And we'd speak the uncovered truth

No fences or traps, no going in circles doing laps
To try and discover if the other truly *gets* us

There'd be nothing more and nothing less
Than these sincere words we'd never forget

But just knowing, just knowing

Friend

You brought me out
Of my own personal darkness
A stormy season of departures
A scarring time
But the time we spent in the cave, we spent
Together
And I know if I'm ever brought back
To a place like that again
You'll be there whatever the weather
And if the comforts of life
Are ever stripped back
What more do I actually need–
Than a friend like you
I just want to thank you

You have put me before yourself
In every way imaginable
In any way that is tangible
For the human heart to comprehend
You've been solid, a promise, honestly honest
You are
The raw real deal and I'm constantly astonished
By the way you love the unpolished me
And know me
Completely
And now when I stare at the remains of the scars
All I can see is

HOPE
And the scope
Of what has been and can still become
You have laughed with me
In the tensest of times
Unleashed my character
When I've been confined to the fine lines
Of who I am and the front I'm trying on

We have cried so much together
With the laughter, love, light of life
The seasons of fight or flight
Where you have tightly wrapped your arms
Around me
Like feathers sheltering me
To not just weather the storm but
Thrive
Like an Eagle to her offspring
You nudged me towards the edge
You showed me that the fear of falling
Was so small in comparison
To the overwhelming joy of soaring
You broke the boundaries, and carried me
You comforted me with the gentle washing of
Words
You defended me with fierce roaring
You gave me a purpose in love, a calling
You called me into
Family, foundation and friendship
What would I do without a friend like you?
I would certainly cease to exist

Or at least my very existence would be
Breathless and pointless
You are the one that has showed me life
And that the palette is deeper, brighter, vaster
Than I ever could have imagined

You are the one that made this fun
I'm flummoxed at the thought of living life without
You
Someone who fought for me
For my attention, sought my soul, spirit and
Protection
You don't withdraw from my gaping neediness
You're not shaken by my shaky weak at the knees
Jesus!
Nothing and nobody else can cut it like you
I'm flummoxed at the thought of living life without
You
Someone who fought for me
For my attention, sought my soul, spirit and
Protection

I owe you e-v-e-r-y-t-h-i-n-g!
So, with every bit of me
Every piece, particle, neuron, atom, cell
Every tear, smile, memory, whisper, shout and yell
Every action, reaction
Response and time to dwell
Every follicle, decision, dream, vision and
Precision
Each ambition, mission, peace, goal and division

Every hurt, all the pain, each wound and the rain
Every season, reason, freedom
Sun Start and completion
Every teaching, every phase
Every year, all my days
I give your grace back in praise
And I thank you for your ways

'Cus they

Are

Better

Than

Mine

!

Dear Beauty

I know nothing prepared you for this
And it's not just what's happened
In recent events   but
It's like you've been isolated
Camped out in exiled tents
For too long
That the idea of hope
For things to recover
Have been suffocated and smothered
Pressed down, repressed, pushed away in the test
That knowing who you are
Is a question mark too big to assess
In the exhausted mess
There've been some dark days
Really dark days
Where you've questioned whether you should
Go on
That the idea of moving forward seems futile
And what's a little while, what's a little bit of time
Gonna change?
If life is possible to hurt in this way
That waking up in the morning is the most
Challenging part of your day
I have a lot to say

But the recurring phrase that won't go away is
This too shall pass
Like all beginnings and ends
The joyous times, the reality, the pretend
The depressed days, tests, frets and each phase
This too shall pass
And while you're in between
The valley of feeling nothing
And shocking pain too real to begin
To explain
Where metaphors of valleys wind you up
Everyday
Along with people trying to encourage you
Through poetry or some way
It doesn't make anything change
Everything I have to say is that
This too shall pass
And it *will*
And you *will* find hope again
And you're not alone
It's important you

Stay!

What if
the things you thought
were too late
actually
start their journey
today?

Seasons

Exhale Vol.2 ONM

Where my hope's been capped
By words that trapped my heart
From tapping into your presence
The doctors room
The grade I didn't make
The relationships I lost
I've learned the very essence of your spirit
Lingers, dwells in the strangest of places
Tasting joy!
In the unexpected
The gutters
Where hope flutters in on wings of spring blooming
You catapult me back to life
Throw me full whack to action
With even just a fraction of your joyful strength
Responding to my cry
You arrive like an avalanche from heaven
Reports that have talked me out
Of living from the abundantly abundant life
You came and made death redundant
You take this bad news
And what appears irreparable
Seemingly irredeemable
Your excitement glows
While the seedling of my faith begins to grow

In this bliss
And you say
Wait till
You see
What I'm
Gonna do
With this

Tell Me What You See

Tell me what you see
He said
Well
I started as cynically as I intended to go on
I see
A vast open space with nothing and nobody
No sounds whirling round no communication
No live plants only cracked ground
I see an empty desert space with no trace of
Anything that can feed me, so hot my veins dried
Out; nothing can bleed from me
The life that left me before you brought me here
And now everything is stuck and it's all too late
What's your plan?
Because I'm starting to think you never had one
Tell me what you see he said
Really?!
I see a
Blanket of clouds overcast but no rain
Shadows from hills no lights it's the same
Trees with no fruit, I'm dizzy and dazed
Hard spikey roots can't be moved
It's the same
It has been over and over again and again

We've been walking for so long
Dried up

What is your plan before I take matters into my
Own hands?
Tell me what you see he said
I told you!
I see a vast open space with nothing
Dried up ground and−
Wait...
There's a leaf and a stem
It's the seed in the cracks of the ground
Taking root
It's alive and it's green and there's sound
And there's fruit
A gentle breeze and a buzz blows a leaf
I hear and I see
Tell me what you see he said
Amidst a desolate derelict weather−beaten
Wasteland so extreme
Afflicted by heat that caused cracks to form in the
Seams of the ground
I see a seed, a stem, a vision of hope
Tell me *who* you see he said

I see you

Deserts

Bounding, leaping, running
The thud thud of my feet was like the beat
Of a drum coming
Raindrops splattered my face and cases of
Hailstones, lacerated patches and places of skin
The opposition
Scratching at my face
The harder it hurt as I gained a greater pace
Legs like propellers
Feet hitting hard, slimy slabs, gripping each step
As if it would never let go
I pelted passed tombstones and graves
With nothing to separate my tears from the rain
I hurdled over diagnosis
Without a second thought to ever look back again
Relentlessly
I put one foot in front of the other
Brain smothered in conquering thoughts
I went on.

Legs began to ache
I found myself caught in a long stretch of
Homelessness
No shelter from my face being slapped by the
Fierce wind
Just endless space
It went on and on
Every time I thought it would come to an end

I could see another hundred miles stretch out
Round the bend
As if there to defend the horizon
Pretending to my exhausted heart that
It'll just be another three steps
Just another three steps
Just another three steps.

Bounding, leaping, running
The thud thud of my feet was like the beat
Of a drum coming
Raindrops splattered my face
As I trudged through mud
This is where I continued to trip, slip, sink and fall
Bones shaking, teeth chattering
As my hands clutched the mud
I crawled and trawled through landscape
That muted the sound
Of the thud of my feet and the call of my cry
I trudged and trudged
Was lost and gave up.

I came round
To the sound of my subconscious
Yelling as if all hell broke loose
It's time to get up
It howled
Giving up are just words

It's an ideologic privilege that doesn't actually
Exist!
There. Is. No. Such. Thing.
By this point I was beaten, battered, scathed and
Bruised but
I fumbled to my feet as I was beginning to feel like
I had nothing to lose
I approached mountains, limping
Bones rattling within me
Legs like worn, rusted propellers, there was no
Sign of life
Just a sign saying
Welcome to the valley of the shadow of death
I could feel the hills icy cold breath
On the back of my neck
As they moved in closer, now clutching my lungs
In one hand
And pushing me down with the other
Whispering
Give up now or I'm gonna find a way to take you
Persisting
I took one step in the sinking mud and slid
Crawling writhing, sliding
The thud thud of my heart was like the beat of
A lost child crying
Grasping and reaching for anything
That could hold me
Pull me back to life
Allow me the luxury of feeling like I was in control
Again
I reached the bottom and slid into the ocean.

Feet first face slapped by the lapping of the waves
Hands flapped, breath gave in an effort to save me
Lungs pushed, water gushed, salty drops through
My eyes
Core broke, spirit crushed as I washed up on the
Shore
I woke.
Sand dunes were soft
Salty eyes now dried
The scorching sun brought life to my eyes
Warmth to my skin
Purified my soul like fire from within
The sound of life travelled far and vast
My feet were rooted in the sand steadfast
I cast my cares and worries to the endlessly rich
Space
And the silence of voices meant distractions were
Erased
In that freedom, I imprisoned myself in hope
Just one tender whisper
Was left gently comforting me

Resting, healing, dreaming
The thud thud of my feet was now a distant
Memory
Leaving
Hot sun shone on my face.
Who knew God would heal in the desert place.

24

Patience

She stayed
She waited
Nothing came
Sat still
Flinching, fidgeting, rocking
Huffing, puffing, sighing, crying
She rested, she waited, she stamped her feet
Burnt out, sedated, in a tantrum
Exhausted
Her fury was fuelled then deflated
It didn't come.
She cursed, she praised
Sometimes skipped, felt waylaid
She stared and gazed and tallied the days
Frustrated and slept
Joked and wept
Then still, it didn't come.
She climbed the walls
She'd forget, waited, changed
Positions
Rearranged
She gauged thoughts
Her mood would fade
She waited and played

And it came

The beautiful, loving, marvellous

Presence
She wasn't the same.

Then

The thing she waited for
Arrived too

But she was only too relieved
For the patience that came

Joy is Coming

"It is not dead. There is still so much more for
You"
I listened to what she said
About her own story
Like strumming a chord, the strings of my heart
Resonated
In tune with each word
Elated
As if my own chest debated
Taking off, light with wings of a bird
Taking flight
It was joy
Hello joy!
Real words
Not a fake fancy of flawed superficial personalities
Dancing in one ear and out the other
With absolutely no substance whatsoever
No deceiving lies of happiness acting clever
Something actually taking root
A glimmer of what's to come
What's already there
Making its home in my heart

Forever

variation video

Heart Balloons

The sound of the sea in the shell in my ears, my
Eyes Like sponges soaking up what appears
Palms sky high with the sand on my skin, peace
Overtakes as my stress levels thin
White beaches reach skies, horizons, the waves
Like diamonds
Colours, split, melt − sunset to sea salt smelt
In chest heart felt.

Pelting down with rain, I run and reach out to the
Rusty back carriage of a train
A stranger's hand grabs mine
Too late to think, moments been, they didn't think
Twice with the familiarity of this routine
Helping me on, hours gone
Feet dangling from the train step
That's my seat fat rain drops on me, release from
What's been the intensified heat
I watch scene meet scene − I look around and my
Heart balloons
And soaks up this longed−for monsoon.

The Moon, like a giant bright white smile in the
Sky Giving light. Silently it plays its song to the
Snow
The quietness grows, the stillness bellows and the
Muted sounds are almost too loud to ignore
The ground sparkles, icy white particles

Locked into each neighbour
Reflecting the lights from the night, the most
Theatrical impractical sight
There for what reason but beauty.

And I'm thinking. That I've been sat here in the
Slums out of a goodness in my heart or some
Helpful duty
With the idea that I could help, I could save, build
Inspire, pave a new way
That I could reach out, remove doubt, bring hope
Water their drought
But they've taught me, caught me out, that my
Western ideas are absurd
Their raw beauty has caused my own mutiny
Against the way
I cake up, a made up, faked up version of me using
Make up, with mascara that would have cost as
Much to save her baby
What's wrong with me!? But they don't condemn
Me, they show me how to love
They teach me songs about hope and being free
They dance in a way that preaches liberty and
Their small amount of food they offer me which
Challenges my perspective on generosity
I let go of what I harboured before, that animosity
I take charge with a new joy that adverts
Are no longer the boss of me
I feel free, a new me
Stepping into what I'm meant to be.

We're stood at the top of the Eiffel Tower
The city lights up voices loud we don't cower
We sip champagne, pull a face as if it's too sour
Join hands like links in chains
And celebrate the year to come
I shut my eyes, breathe in
I'm literally overwhelmed with fun.

I'm getting a brand new sun tan on the top of
In the heart of
In the midst, amongst the beauty of
New Zealand
Plane rising, sky diving, long journeys
I'm driving, loud music, it's booming
Sing song sing along
Barbecue burning, pass the tongs
Singing. Phone not ringing
Silence.
What a virtue, can't believe this is happening
Can't believe this is true
Water skiing, just being set me free, climbing trees
Eating honey with the bees
You're you
I'm me
They're them
Never been so content, never been so happy
Doing Flamenco, eating tapas, in the Big Apple
Watching Rappers
Breakers breaking – my heart raking it in

And then

I sit back and snap out of it.

I realise it's raining outside. There's a mess of
Paper on my desk.   I let out a
Small laugh
I'm staring
At the debt of my huge overdraft
My time will come.

                              I will do
                         These Things

Blood Red Thread

The threads weaved in and out with joy and dread
Peaks and troughs, life and death
Coarse metallic splintered through soft mesh while
Colourful shades stayed
Accumulating pictures and shapes
In the complex and beautiful mess
Threads of lies weaved into confessions
Threads of aggression blistered repeatedly
Until It faded needlessly. Threads unravelled.
One needle pin prick for the start of each colour
One needle pin prick bled the mesh
Like blood from flesh
One needle pin prick for the start of a season
One needle pin prick painfully pierced a reason
I looked at the tapestry and it was clear
Some parts didn't start as the Artist's plan
But
Finished with deeper, embellished shades
That added to the picture, the waves
Then the very weight of depression
I don't mean to be cliché but
Some dark greys, I guess represented oppression
Reality looked too hard, too real
Too close and exposed
The emotions; confusing
Where some threads started loosening
While others

Profusely poured parts that started a season
Which prepared wounds for healing
The golden threads
They were marvellous, extravagant
Made up of so many intertwined situations
Knitted a picture of life's beautiful complications
The golden threads looked *worth it*
I could just about make out why
The Artist's hand stitched this story
It was perfect
Then,
I took a step closer
And the colours got bolder
Deeper, darker, some vivid, brighter
Some leaving faded scars, others like sticky tar
Imprisoned behind bars

The heart of the tapestry
Bled through vibrant threads acting as arteries
Each one entwining a verse that bled into a story
I stood, close, stuck
At the mourning and grief, the trials
And feelings of fleeting hope
Dashed for a while
The feelings of forgotten
The threads, dripping, leaking
Almost looking rotten
Until
I stood back
And that's when I could see
The salty sea blues

The yellow rays of truth
The comforting compassions of red
The playful pinks
The galvanising greens
And no longer a single woven thread
But the bigger picture, which was far prettier
Creating and forming a stunning view
Of you and your intention behind it
That echoed a story, a print
Showing from start to finish
A blood – red – thread
Through every trial
And every tribulation
Through e–v–e–r–y bit of suffering
And identities authentication
I saw the real reason
And final conclusion
For which it all added to
Like a perfectly thought out equation
I saw that after depression, came elation
That grief surrendered to a joyous
Whirling dance
I was captured by the detail
Entranced by the view
Romanced by the fruit
From the start of the seed
Which grew through the mesh
Engulfing my heart's flesh
The weaving of life taking its toll
Creating a beautiful picture
A goal

Making total sense
On that mesh
Life was depicted
When I took a step
Back

And embraced
The bigger picture.

The Wait is Over

A Christmas Poem

I'm at home in this little old room, cleaning clothes
Doing what I usually do
When I feel something in the atmosphere change
Like Something so familiar yet strange had
Arranged to visit me
I shake it off – I'm just not thinking clearly, it's
Early and I carry on cleaning
But then
I feel the tangible, delightful, heaviness that
Perhaps this instinct is real, and I need to turn
Around
Like humanity is waiting on me with its weighty
Anticipation while heavenly hosts are watching
Curiously
By now I feel so differently
There's no way there's no change and that this
Little old room will ever look the same when I look
Behind me
So I turn and see sheets of an immense, intense
Incandescent popping luminous light
Shimmering blades ablaze with rays of glazed
Glittering tidal waves washing right through me
In brilliant radiance, yet simultaneously
Punctured by shock, rocked to my core
Still as I'd ever been yet trembling between
Breaths 'Greetings you who are highly favoured
You have nothing to fear, the one true God is near'

I watch for the words to unravel from his tongue
He begins to explain I'll give birth to a son
That the wait is over, and he is the One
Terrified to speak but filled with an undying need
To say
'You must be deceived, there is no way I could
Have conceived if you get what I mean?
I mean what will people say? How will they treat
Me? Would anyone even believe me?'
The anxieties that race right through me
Halt at his words
'Holy... Spirit'
And that's all I needed
Just his name, to hear it
Jesus!
Throughout the whole world's brokenness
Jesus, in every diagnosis
Jesus, in every unsalvageable situation
Jesus, in our own humanity's devastation
Jesus!
YES! Yes! I accept anything
For the name of Jesus

What if
there's more to you than
you imagine?

This Little Girl

This little girl wants to leap high
Grow a propeller, take off and fly
She won't let another moment
Opportunity pass her by
As time ticks

She doesn't want to get high off empty kicks or
Merely, complete a 'to do before she dies'
Covered with ticks
Nor does she want to get stuck−in−a−rut of acting
Lovesick

She wants to take the first brick and build
The parts of her life
That will fulfil others with new life
Joy that is refreshing, that breaks the chains
She'll boldly step into darkness
Paint new colours, inspired by her Artist
Oppressing chains will fall

Traps will be in tatters
As joy is flung and splattered on the walls
New life, new life is born
Every unintentional, internal vow will be ruined at
Its core

As she asks for more
New life! New life!

This place is dead

But even death has to end

And the lies can only sink under the surface and
Pretend
Hiding, cowering
Applying poor excuses to defend itself
Whereas the truth does not depend on an enemy
                    But it stands alone
On solid ground
That's where this little girl
Wants to be found

Dear Heart

You've been through undeserved pain
The 4am heart ache
The questions
That made your heart break
On the path of how come
And the lake of uncertainty
The fake dagger
That blamed you
Enflamed
Your watery eyes
The fed-up sighs
And of course
The questions why?
But I'm here
With a surge in my spirit
To tell you something
Now
Because I feel it
Undeniably–
If you knew your own
Hope
Inside out
It would blow your
Mind
Crush your doubts
You'd find
The mouthful

Of life that threatens
Will
POP!
The smallest of bubbles
The gentlest mist
That won't last
Like lies
That twist perspective fast
Don't fret
Loose them
Free them
To be caught
In his net
As it's cast out
In the morning
With fresh mercies
The bringer of life
And destroyer of Curses
He loves you
He loves you
He loves you
When you face the army ahead
Feeling alone
Dig your feet deep in the ground
Turn around
See you have the backing
Of mountains,
All the oak trees of the Earth
The highest tree tops
Each animal and the result
Of her birth

The stars and the sun
Burning fiercely fearlessly
The ocean, cliffs and sky
Boldly declaring
That he is ruler, in charge of your life
And he is on your side
Confide your grief with Him
And ride your life within
The home of his heart

He Loves you!

He Loves you!

He Loves you!

Thunder

My heart bleeds for you
Loves and hurts for you
Hands weave lungs breathe
Home leaves for you
Soul longs for you
Core splits in two for you
Body moved spirit grew
Life lives for you
Strife, grief
Shrinks in you
You nurture me
Perfecting me
Poured in me, always
Changing me for the world to see
Yet teaching me to walk humbly
Broke the sky crashed clouds
Cliffs crumbling
Thunder rumbling
Love tumbling
Whispers to shout
Crash clouds
Your thundering
Winds blundering
Looks stunning
In the running of
Your creating
Elating the world
We're waiting for you,
Are you coming?

Real

Arms stretched; fists clenched
Examining every wall of skin, every birth mark
Freckle and her twin
Sizing up the veins now larger than life
Counting every hair, now counting it twice
Advice from my mind
Is it on my side? Is *she* being too kind?
Cut the fringe to hide the spots, shave the skin
Disguise the dots
A photo, my sight, reflection, what's what?
Lost amidst the confusion
In dispersed illusion – is she Alien? Am I Human?
Or am I just a girl who wasn't ready for
Photoshop?
See, what it seems to be, is our bodies aren't sewn
We're seamless you see
With your eyes
But our bodies in their natural habitats are faced
With lies
So, it's time for me to choose to be wise
And use my mind for the truth
I'm not being kind. The. Truth. Is. Real
Arms stretched that day, I made the choice
I'm going to live life *this* way
My veins named *too visible*
Have my life running through them
This is how I choose to view them
So, I'll use my words as tools not abuse them

Look at me!

My skin, the world wouldn't describe as perfection
Is my boundary, my wall, my physical protection
Don't think about your younger days
And how you miss them
Wrinkles display beauty, life, experience and
Wisdom
Look at your scars, the way they say *you* survived
And your stretch marks are evidence you carried a
Life
From now on I reflect the new perspective
I elected
That beauty is never about the truth that we
Let get infected
When we agreed to believe it's all about glamour
Or how much Botox we can get injected
I won't be misdirected by the lies that waste time
Because
Ugliness
Can only spill from a heart or a mind, which is a
Choice
It's never external
Appearance won't last and can't be eternal
So why waste time?
                    When love lasts

Beautiful Brain

Redefine beauty
Your brain goes where you take it
Purpose, no mistake

Oxytocin

Aka Landscapes

Beautiful landscapes
Painted across the drapes, spaced across the place
Of This world
Iced mountains
Some, too deadly to conquer
Though they remain untouched they're beautiful
For something in all their splendour
The somewhat spontaneous growth of plants
Contain and adhere t'
So much mathematical order like
Space, leaves, staggered trees, spiralling
Permitting Optimum sunlight
Are they exhibiting a fight for life?
Or are they exhibiting how to be *gloriously*
Content?
Responding to the great fiery star
An order to photosynthesise
To breed their own life, creating O2
So we can breathe in our life absorbing that too
Contorting, contracting and growing
The tubular branches soaking up, breathing deep
Within the soil of our chests, eventually
Microscopic
Air rushes into tiny sacs and pockets
Without our brains even bringing it to our
Consciousness

As eighty-six billion electrically excitably charged
Cells well up with chemical signals
Firing them up, so that we can speak, we can tell
Hold hands, perceive and believe
So we can walk, we can talk, we can swallow
Breathe and see
Eyes detecting and converting lights into
Electrical, chemical impulses
Distinguishing shapes and colours
As we take pleasure in the magnificent lights
Bending in the sky's horizons
Illuminating the droplets as streaks of colour
Appear and bend with the Earth's curve
But say our world was a little to the left
Or shifted off course to the   right
The magnetic force wouldn't be   right
We'd be exposed to harmful radiation
Freeze from the cold or not enough light
We *will* die without the light
We are in just the right place at just the right time
I'm not superstitious
Scientifically our planets and stars are so
Perfectly aligned that the fight for life in these
Conditions means we can survive
We can choose
To exist, or live an abundant life
I don't have many answers, and the ones I do
Some would disagree
But we got here out of intimacy
The most physically close humans can be
There was around a one in forty million chance

It would be *you* that was born
Two little cells made you
                    Look at you!
Oxytocin and Dopamine
Are two hormonal chemicals released during birth
Which means
Mothers connect with their babies
And a euphoric state of love literally courses
Through their veins
A love chemical that conquers
The sheer exhaustion and labour pains
A love that conquers pain
There is so much we can explain

But *why*
        Do we need to love
                        And receive it
    All the same?

You Are

Hello you
This is you
Speaking to you
On your good day
So you know
If your confidence and esteem
Whistles away in the way off wind
Where you find
It won't be where you left it
(And we know that can happen)
When you see I'm right about that
You'll know you can trust me with this
You
Are
BRILLANT!
You were made and created using
BRILLIANCE!
And wait!
Don't listen to them for a minute
Listen to me, trust me
You have it woven, embedded, threaded
Deep down in your bones
Sewn into the fabric of your soul
Written in the membranes that make you
You
Written in your history and memories
Unwinding through your infirmities
That you have chosen to pour your spirit

Through
Like Niagara Falls
Powered by a jet propeller force
Better than any wonder of the world
It's yours!
Sticks and stones will break your bones if
They're thrown hard enough
But words with your permission
Will take pieces of your soul
So, hold on and protect it, but
Do not grow a thick skin
You'll only train yourself to stop feeling
                           Thoughts!
Sitting in the organ in your head
While you're sitting thinking about what
They said, when someone made you feel like
You're a failure
You'll never make it, you'll never break into
What you dreamt of
Just know that your very anatomy
Defies so many impossibilities and the
Atrocities that have been flung at you
Undeserved
Insecurities unearthed
New issues about your appearance birthed
Covered up pain found and turned
Like dried mud stuck under stones
Rejected, bullied, trolled
Brokenness unfolds and soon

You believe everything you've been told
And you've forgotten what you had once
Known
Don't be hard on yourself
That's what anyone in this position would do
And by this position
I mean
Receiving the pettiest of comments that
Have cut, stuck, left cemented, lamenting
Bending the truth about you
When the truth is
YOU ARE BRILLIANT!
That fact that you are still here
No matter what kind of trembling mess
You feel like you've crumbled into
                    Or
Meltdowns you've liquidised into
You. Are. Still. Here.
And you are still brilliant!
You've shown that you refused to let go
You're still here and you are still
BRILLIANT!
And me?
Well I'm so proud of you!

Twigs

I look at each twig laced
Encrusted encased in the night's frost
Lost amidst a whole universe of creation
Each sunrise, every morning, the Earth's elation
Not one thing the same as another
Not one thing twinned with the other
All uniquely brilliant, a masterpiece
My eye's feast as one hundred and eighty billion
Cells
Circle in the contours of the outdoors
Absorbed by every pore, every blink of the eye
Every touch of the skin
A new picture as the sea mimics the sky
Every move of the moon pulls the force of the
Tide
Creatures
Each perfectly formed feather
Enabling the bird to fly
Every particle gliding, sliding,
Forming a new thing
Bringing life
Stars that burned up and disappeared
For hundreds of years
Have finally appeared in the Earth's stratosphere
The foggy atmosphere

Heavily waiting, settling, sedating the air
To a heavy dampened state
Hanging over the beaches
Left untouched
Out of those tucked up in beds' reach
Each shell painted with a different marking
Each season changing by the bright
And the darkening
Each season changing by the bright
And the darkening
As winter is embarking
On its next freeze

If Love Was a Colour

If love was a colour would it be red
Straight forward and cut clean?
Would it be pink like all the cliché hearts
And Valentine cards?
Would it be mixed with green
Having envy slip in unseen?
Would it be a black and white film, romantic in
Every scene?
Or would it be mixed up
Every colour under the sun
Every shade visible to the eye?
Would it be the tears birthed, warming the sides of
Your face
As they slide, through every ride of nostalgia
The present and hope
Every thought, feeling, act, compromise, sacrifice
Splattered at a canvas
Colours of life thrown with all abandon, crammed
In
So you're required to take ten feet back just to
Take it all in
And still be unable to figure it out
Is love so simple that to apply it, it is to *just* love
Or is it so complex in the sense
That it *is* so simple

That it's best described through
Life's patterns, joys, tribulations and trials
Through a friend for life, brother and sister
Child and parent, husband and wife
Do we depict it with a picture of a sunset and a
Romantic quote?
Or do we depict it with a moment
Where we let a stranger go before us
Is it a passive act of whispering sweet nothings
To make us feel good, using common flattery
Or is it 'liking' someone's selfie with a heavy sense
Of apathy
Or
Is it the urge to chip in when you see someone
Short of their bus fare by 10p?

If love was a story would it be what
Hollywood brings to the TV
A neatly tied plot begins at A and ends at B
Would it be a sonnet, or play asking
To be or not to be
Or would it be a history, present and hope
Of someone loving
You and me unconditionally
Someone who didn't owe the world anything, yet
Draws close

We have a longing for love, to not do this on our
Own
To share the rhythm of the day, the notes of the
Night

And the tones of our lives
We are created using threads of relationships
To be with and alongside

In the grief and rocky rides
Oceans of joy lapping with the tides of life
Belly laughing till we cry
To stand through thick and thin
Side by side
In all the colours and stories and patterns of life

So, if love was one colour, I don't think
It would really be love
Not unless you can paint it with all of the above
Using a palette
Of patience, kindness, justice, forgiveness,
Sacrifice, faith, hope and endurance
Through every circumstance

If love *was* a colour
It would be one of many
That would create a masterpiece

He Did it For Me

An Easter Poem

He's got rips in his body
And his eyes are crying red
The thorns are digging in
'Cus they're wrapped round his head
His face is disfigured
His hands and feet have holes in
He's doing this for me
To pay the debt for my sin

He's falling to the floor
'Cus of the weight of the cross
He's saying *Please live life*
I'll take the loss
His body is ruined
He's covered in red stripes
Close to death's door
Yet he's *still* the living light!

The Soldiers are gambling
The Thief behind is taunting
The shouts and cries from the
Crowd are completely haunting
I'm saying *JESUS! Don't do this*
I'm not perfect, I'll sin again!
He says *Daughter, I love you, I*
Forgive you my friend
The clouds are getting heavy

People start to disperse
I look up at his face
And his suffering gets worse
My heart starts to shout
I've sinned, I'll sin again
I'm sure
He looks at me with eyes that say
Daughter, you are worth dying for.

Eloi Eloi lama sabachthani?
He says with his last breath
And I fall to my knees
My heart overwhelmed
All I could do was cry
As the Son of man wanted me to live
So he chose to die.

The ground started to break
The Temple's curtain was torn
They had all laughed and jeered at him
The king of Jews with the thorns!

But, he came back.
After three days dead.
Just like he said
He was resurrected
Victory is won he paid our debt
More real, than reality
He's living right now
Given us life to live in abundance
Let's show the world how

What if
this moment counts
for more than you thought?

Once Upon a Time

Once upon a time a young girl died, she went up
To heaven and looked in the eyes of the
Most High for the first time
He looked at the girl and said

Daughter, not yet there's still more for you
Your life is all set

The sound of his words surged through her soul
She felt complete, delighted and whole
She made herself comfy and didn't want to move
He cherished that moment
And said

Daughter
I love you

It was as if she'd always known, but for the first
Time she really knew. She spoke with depth and
Truth when she said

Father
I love you too

He responded
You've been here a while
But no time has changed on Earth
I'm sending you back to fulfil your purpose

She cried
Father, please no! My life was all set
But I'm here with you now and besides
We've just properly met

His heart warmed and words danced from his
Mouth. He assured her heart to wash away every
Doubt

Daughter, Beloved, Significant
Don't forget
I'm with you on earth as much as you let

Stamping her feet and waving her arms
She quietly growled
She threw a little tantrum, until she finally spoke
Aloud

Up here, I've not thought, one thought of what
People think of me
Life there, people stare, at my every insecurity

My perforated heart starts to shred and tear
On earth
I'm unsatisfied and I'm just not content

You, Most High
Know most
That hearts are oppressed

I get stressed, tense and depressed
I can't escape fear and life feels like one big test

His heart glowed knowing she was showing
Vulnerability
But it broke into pieces with humanity's chosen
Fragility

My Daughter you're precious
I've kept your every tear
For now, look at your life
I'll give you brand new eyes
To see clearer

She looked through his eyes and saw her life on
Earth
To the moment she died from the day of her birth
The people, they loved her more than she knew
And everyone's image was beauty
She could see that was true

She had no reason to fear
Her words had power; Angels stood around her
So tall they would tower

See, your life is good
When you look with these eyes
Continue to use them and you'll be surprised

She sat
Still as she'd ever been, witnessing
The intricate details of her life
Watching closely, every scene

She saw as she was led by a hand into safety
Excitedly she cried out as if watching TV

When danger was lurking, your hand came and
Saved me!

Wherever she was, each corner she turned
An intense fire of love
Surrounded her and burned

Unaware, as she went about her days
Angels filled her rooms, street, work and
Sang out in praise

She could see her gifts, so huge in her heart
But only a fragment she used
When she worked at her art

Father, why is this, my talents I waste?
I've got a whole banquet, yet I only gave a taste

Fear my Dear
His voice soothed as he held her
It imprisons my children when they really could
Prosper

She thought about her life
And how quickly it went
How she merely attempted her calling
From the Most High she was sent

Father, I repent
If I went again
I wouldn't relent

But what would equip me and how would I know
That I am truly loved and already have it all so?

My word, you must read it
Absorb it and eat it
My love
Well, it's evident in the Son and the rain
So, search for me in your trials
Your joy and the mundane

Something stirred the girl when she heard his
Words
A frustration of debating life's big questions just
Blew up and burst!

But where are you God, when right now
You're not in the physical!?

It's pretty hard trusting in Someone
Who is clearly invisible

I don't understand the suffering people go through
When you say that you love us
How can that be true?

His eyes met hers to the deepest part of her core
She resumed reverence but encountered the truest
Love in the form of warmth

I will never leave you
When you feel washed out
Dried up, broken and alone
I will never leave you
When everything you know has disappeared
And you can't do it alone
Nothing will ever separate my love for you
When you're tangled in a web of anxiety
Crushed in stress
If your marriage is falling apart
If your life is a mess
If you're struggling to get your head
Above a sea of debt
If you can't even begin to remember
The definition of 'blessed'
And when life has just felt
Like it's test, after test, after test

After test

After test

I will never leave you
When you're sick
And think it might never end
When you're grieving
And heart broken
From losing a friend
When you're depending on
Each
New
Moment
To give you news of hope
When the thought of
Death is far more tempting
And you're not sure how to cope
I will never leave you!
When you're surrounded
By good news and friends
Riding a high and soaking up
The colourful complexities
Of life
Dancing in simplicities
And secure in your
Necessities
They came from me
I will never leave you!
I will never leave you!
I will never leave you!
So you want to see me on Earth?
Well,
When you're in the world
And you love another soul

Regardless of
What they've done
Who they are
Or what they owe
Clearly
Obviously
Gloriously
When you love another
That's where you'll see me

Her time in Paradise was over for now
She shut her eyes
And knelt down before the Almighty and bowed
She opened her eyes
And returned to the mundane
But when she looked around
She knew this time
It wouldn't be the same
She took a deep breath in
Thinking and appreciating
All of the people she loved
And a golden flash burst before her
Reminding her
Of her time
Up above

If No One Spoke of Them

Would you still use your gifts
If no one spoke of them?

Would you still go back to that place of joy
Where you lost track of time
Every time
You stepped into your gift

If you never broke the seal of fame
Gathered riches, saw your name
In lights

If no one cared, no one wanted to know
Would you go back to that place of joy
Where you lost track of time

Would you still pursue and hunger
For those hours on end
Where life suspends
And you would defend
Any moment that you could tend
To your gifts to see them grow

Because every time you work at it
You begin to sew a harvest
Of pure delight in me

If it was just me

If it was just me who saw
Who watched every moment
Gazed in suspense and delight
Satisfied, content and fired-up
As you blazed away at
That thing you loved

If it was just me
Who called encore
And brought
The house down with applause
Mouthed your songs word for word
If it was just me that listened and heard

Because when you do it
Use it
Get lost in it
When it's just you and no one can see
My heart flips out of my chest
My gaze engaged with everything
You do
Locked in wonder
My thoughts applaud you
Cheer you!

Would you use your talents if it was only
I that spoke of them?

Bridge The Gaps

Fill in the slots and the slats
The empty spaces, nooks, crannies and gaps
Fill the blank canvas, the boxes and sacks
Fill someone's heart, the empty purse and the
Cracks
Cover the brick wall, the roof and the board
Keep moving relentlessly always towards
The goal
Sew the tiny seeds that make gardens and trees
Be the step closer to setting someone free
Never despise the day of small beginnings
And don't be in it to just count up your winnings
Fill in the lines, the colours and dots
Keep asking questions, the whys and the whats
Be the solution and your own growing evolution
For all the right causes start a revolution
Stand in the gap to reduce your pollution
Be the house to the homeless
And the food distribution
Because if we no longer take a step back and
Rather
Move forward to fill the gaps
We will carry the baton where the politicians let us
Down
Where the systems in place have obscured the
Pace
At which we need to move

To prove that our society can be loving
Can be helping
Can be creative, illuminating the dreams of
The next Generation
When we stand in our station
Of doing our bit
And become more about the foundation and less
About the winning
More about travelling the journey well
Than the end destination
Less about making money run from taps
If we are the people who will step up and
Bridge the gaps

Today

Today could be better than you think
Take a deep breath
let it sink

Uproot the anxious seeds
And sew the thankful shapes
That deserve a place in the cutouts
Of your current situation
Then praise some
Today is a gift beyond your imagination
Today is a place for you to play
To enjoy the way the that you were made
To embrace your day in ways that will never fade
But be an imprint
In the story of how you made a change
Today you changed someone's day
That enabled them to say these words
To pass back to you
Today you made everything okay
Today you made it
Tomorrow
Well
Tomorrow's looking bright too

A Poet's Song

You are the early birdsong
On a summer morning
The vivid colours blooming in opened flowers
The smell of adventures in barbecue evenings
The soft clouds sweeping a blue sky clean
Of yesterday
You are the good soil fresh each morning
For the sowing of futures
We can only begin to know
You are the warmth of sunrays
In the haze of heat waves
You're the strong oak tree
Quenching the desire for shade
The hiding place in winter; the resting place
You are the sound of a trickling river
Glimmer, glitter emitting
The sound of bashing rocks
Gently tapped cleaned and swept
By the washing
You are majesty
Pouring
Dripping
Warming oil
The good soil
You are the filling for lonely spaces
Empty places
Waiting for love
Inviting of love

A Time for Mourning

Why didn't the traffic stop
The clocks stop
The shops shut
The News pause
The birds still
The train halt
The silence move
When news arrived
That you
Arrived in Paradise
That you exhaled your last full stop
Why didn't everything else
Stop!?
Why is it still moving
Why is the world deluding itself
By carrying on
Why am I expected
To take the puzzled piece of me
And place it neatly in the puzzle
Of routines
Work, showers, brushing teeth
And all kinds of normality
Why are people walking in streets
Commuting to the office
Drinking coffee

Like nothing ever happened
No one knows it seems
Just me
Just me in this grief
Even though so many mourn you
It feels like just me in this grief

*What if
it's all been
taken care
of?*

Anxiety Bye!

Every now and again
You rear your ugly little head
And tell me that instead of dancing
I've got to lie down
Instead of laughing
I should be grieving, heaving, thoughts, solutions
To problems you forgot to mention
Will likely never happen
You try tapping into my subconscious
With flashcards of monstrous promises
To ensure a constant consciousness
Of your pompous and obnoxious torrents
Did you miss
I only listen to one promise
Streamlined to only accept one covenant
So with this renewed vision
Recycled mind
This new system
I'll use my sight for truth and blind the waffle you
Rattle on about all day
You don't take me by surprise anymore
In fact
You've become entirely drab, dull and boring
I'm going to snore overtime you talk
And focus on the glory
Because there is more, so much more than you
Can offer me
I scoff at your sneaky, thief like ways

Proper robber in the night I look to daylight and
Praise
Because your hold on me
Is only as much as I allow
I'm in control
There's the door

Buh-Bye!

Peace

Quick fling back
To the Mediterranean Sea
Paddling, emerging breaking the divide
Where liquid meets sky in the sparkling sunshine
Feeling the warmth bounce
Reflecting out to a personal spotlight
That no one else will find out about
This is just my moment
And it doesn't matter
What's back at the sand
As I disband the attached anxiety
While I watch first hand
The planned variety of leafy textures
Adjacent to crunchy cliffs
Feeling drunk with peace
Yet simultaneously
Sobered by the beauty, tipsy
On the lack of duty
Swirling around me like little whirlpools of rest
Carrying away the little burdens and tests
While light hits my face
And the taste of salty air can't be compared
So, I don't
Because this moment seems to care
And I don't

Handing it Over

I'm handing it over
My cards, my keys
My cash, take it
Please
My successes
Regresses
My pros, cons and
Defeat
I'm stepping, bowing
Down
From the pride
I named *Elite*
I'm giving up, giving
In
As you can see
I well and truly
Am beat
[beat]
I'm handing it over
The shoes from my
Feet
The hat from my
Head
The place where
I go to sleep

Where I lay down in
Bed

I give you the cereal
From my bowl
My titles
My job role
I give you
My reputation
My down days
My joy and elation
I give you my truth
My lies
My boasts and
Fabrications
I give you my
Thoughts
My desires
My dreams for the
Nation
I give you my art
My heart
My imagination and
Creation

And you say

I want your heart
I want you
To be wooed

By my creation
I call it my art
I want your heart
To pound
At the thought
Of you being
Thought of
Before the start
I want you to look
To me for protection
To know
That I am not
Religious
But I pour out *all* my
Affection
I want to defend you
And hold you
After all
It was I that moulded
You
I want you to be
Blessed
I want you
To take Shelter in me
And find rest
Child, it is I that
Calls you blessed

I want you to
Search for me
Seek me, find me and
Pursue me
I pursue you
The very depths of
You
Your core
Every time you
Look to Me
I say
Come
Get to know me more
I command every
Heavy weight
To fall off you
Every burden and
Chore
And in you
I breathe life
I breathe light
I breathed galaxies
Into existence
And I say, *you* child
Are a beautiful sight
With you

I am pleased

The Garden

In the house
Rooms unlit
Curtains cobwebbed across windows
The chairs around the table gained
Dustless shadows
Floorboards moulded with their photograph

In the house
Rooms unlit
The pipes are dry and not even a creak or sigh
From the doors undone

In the house
Rooms unlit
Nobody sat by the table, opened the book
Pulled a drawer or swept the soot

Nobody pushed the door, dirtied the floor

The dust gathered for company
In the house
In the house
Rooms unlit
Particles hovered caught in streaks

Chess piece stuck, the insects left
But

In the garden
Life springs, tides of colours wash
Refreshing changes across
Endless movement of skies and plants
In the garden

Is life.

Thought Processes

We need balance
We need to breathe in and out
Such intricate minds
The little finds in life
That we let define us
I think about how enormous Space is
And how little my mind is
I think about the way I respond to kindness
I grieve at the smallest insult
It swings round and catapults
Previous pain that's affected me
Where people have rejected me
Or neglected me
Even on the smallest scale

I think about how the sun is so big
It makes me feel insignificant
But then I think
The sun is so big for little us
Surely

We are significant

Perspectives

It is only in the silence
That I can hear words loud and clear
It is only in the silence
Where I am completely removed from fear

It is only in the frozen time
When perspective takes its shape
It is only in the frozen time
When I am truly wide awake

It is only in the stillness
That the willingness rises up
It is only in the willingness
That fulfilment fills my cup

It is only in the cup
Where I can receive, receive and pour
It's only if I keep it *to* myself, that I'll dry out and
Become poor

It is only with the poor
Where life's richest gifts are sown
And only in the sowing where we can ever begin to
Grow

*What if
no matter what
everything is going to be
okay?*

Even If

Even if my hopes are dashed
And the results come out
As an unexpected disappointment
Crashing from the sky

I will remember
Who breathed the sky into existence
Who it was that created giant orbs of fire
That spectators on Earth
Would look up and admire
The gentle glimmer

I will remember who it was that planted
The abundance of greens
I will remember who it was
That miraculously, spectacularly
Spoke cells into being
And organised them in places and ways
To create me

I will remember who pressed 'GO'
On my heart and washed blood through my veins
Who knit me
Planned me
Wrote out everyday
In a story before me

I will know it was you
It is you
Every day, every good thing is you
Even if it's not as I orchestrate
I know that the one who made the sky
The trees and all living things
Made me and is with me
Even if it's not as I planned
I know you planned to never leave me

What If?

What if?
There is more to you than you imagine
What if?
There's purpose behind your passion
That knits so perfectly, weaving into a tapestry
Of other people's lives
What if?
You were fashioned for such a time as this, exist
Like you matter more than you give yourself credit
For
What if?
This morning, when you woke up
You were called for living
What if?
The things you thought were too late
Actually, start their journey today
What if?
You aren't lost
What if?
You're moving in the exact direction you're meant
To
That each step forward, each subtraction and
Fraction of a pace never lacked
And you're in the exact right place in the race
What if?
Fate is a waste of time

What if?
The pathways were prepared
But today you have a choice
What if?
We're running out of time
What if?
Your voice is important and contorts the way
Others perceive life to be
What if?
Every time you spoke you had a choice to speak
Hope into another person's soul
What if?
The goal is simpler than you think
What if?
It's all been taken care of
What if?
It's the little things you enjoy
That are some of the biggest gifts you've ignored
And
What if?
This moment counts for more than you thought
Before you heard me say
What if?
And
What if?
No matter what
Everything
Is
Going
To
Be okay!

I Woke up in The Jungle

Consciousness coming round
To a cacophony of sound
This time bit by bit, biting my lip
Waiting for the first hit
But that isn't it, there isn't one
Release tension from my limbs, joints, hips
Hands back together
Heart back together, but it hurts
A bruised fruit too painful to hold
When I felt it crumble, I hadn't adjusted
My understanding
When spirits are crushed
What remains is gold dust
The light cracked through leaves
Pouring in my skin drinking it in
Surrounded by the safety of tall trees
Like Angels in armies protecting me
I can see!
I can see the light!
And its beauty
Powerful pink petals
And neon yellows
Frilled coats over stems
Sheets of intense incandescent
Popping luminous lights

Shimmering raindrops on
Stalks and blades ablaze
With glittering colours in tidal waves
Washing through my broken heart
Like a cracked open stone
Consumed in the bottom of the ocean
You're there
I see you
In brilliant radiance
Scintillating dazzling echoes of
Vibrant sounds, songbirds singing me back
Kicking life into my ear drums
I'm here present
Nature's choir clothing the world in
Worship and adoring awe
As my rib cage swings open
Like an unlocked door
And bit by bit it is all restored
His strength oozing through my arteries
Intact stronger than palm trees
And succulent smells of everything I can now tell
In every sense of the journey
Weaving into a story as a healed answer
Because
I woke up in the jungle
And came back to life

When I Look up at The Sky

When I look up at the sky
It doesn't hurt anymore
The amount of times
It would remind me
Of arriving first thing
In the morning
Amidst exciting flights of
What ifs
And little did yesterday know
These emotional highs
Beautiful sights
Where lights ignited
Rewrites of paths
I couldn't dream up
Seamless divides from
One story to the next
I turned the page
To what felt like a
Fight for life
Emotionally
Where broken me
Lay in A&E

Crying through eyes that so badly wanted to see
But you picked up the debris of me
Sewing me gently with soothing words
That didn't need eyes to hear
Or a voice to listen
Never encouraged a thought to fear
Or a broken stone to glisten
You just let me be
While you pieced me back together
When I look up at the sky
It
Doesn't
Hurt
Anymore

It's Time

So,
Your heart's been through a blender
Your body's taken such a knock
That you're starting to question life's agenda
Your finances are virtually non-existent
And debt is persistently hanging over your head
Love feels distant
And you're just desperately searching for
Some assistance
And purpose in your existence
Because all you want right now is
To resist the pain
And understand why
Things have been so consistently hard

I get it
I'm with you
I understand more than you know
And I came here today to tell you
Everything is going to be okay

The pain is *going* to decrease
And the peace will increase
As each day you power through a new leaf of life
And your belief will see relief
And dreams, desires that were hidden in your
Heart

Will catch an unexpected spark and explode with
Light

You're gonna do things that once frightened you
And this ceaseless fearlessness that was sown
During this trial
Will grow indefinably
Undeniably you will know yourself!
What was once a hurting, broken down gutter in
Your life
Will be the very thing that catapults you into the
Things
You didn't know were possible
Because they weren't
But they are
Now

You better get ready!
Although you thought you missed your chance
And think what should have been
Will remain in the past
And is no more than a glance over your shoulder
You're wrong about that
This is your new beginning
And you needed all of that
So that you never have to back track
Instead you can stack the past like bricks

And follow the path
To live at last
To the full
So
Are you ready?
It's time
Be ready!
Because it's time
Look forward, only look behind to remind yourself
That the task ahead will never outgrow
The strength behind
So,
Are you ready?
It's time

Want to learn a simple exercise to write a poem in ten minutes?

Positive Poetry www.janeymcleod.com

Want More Poems?

Atoms iSci

Real ONM

Baby Steps

Remember
The Sea

What If? ONM

Hindsight

Being Honest